WORLDVIEW GUIDE

THE PICTURE OF DORIAN GRAY

Marcus Schwager

canonpress
Moscow, Idaho

Published by Canon Press
P.O. Box 8729, Moscow, Idaho 83843
800.488.2034 | www.canonpress.com

Marcus Schwager, *Worldview Guide for The Picture of Dorian Gray*
Copyright © 2019 by Marcus Schwager.
Find the Canon Classics version of the book at www.canonpress.com/books/
canon-classics.

Cover design by James Engerbretson
Cover illustration by Forrest Dickison
Interior design by Valerie Anne Bost and James Engerbretson

Printed in the United States of America.

Scripture taken from the New King James Version®. Copyright © 1982 by
Thomas Nelson. Used by permission. All rights reserved.

Library of Congress Cataloging-in-Publication Data:
Schwager, Marcus, author.
The Picture of Dorian Gray worldview guide / Marcus Schwager.
Moscow, Idaho : Canon Press, [2019]
LCCN 2019011344 | ISBN 9781944503949 (paperback : alk. paper)
LCSH: Wilde, Oscar, 1854-1900. Picture of Dorian Gray.
Classification: LCC PR5819 .S39 2019 | DDC 823/.8—dc23
LC record available at https://lccn.loc.gov/2019011344

A free end-of-book test and answer key are available for download at
www.canonpress.com/ClassicsQuizzes

19 20 21 22 23 24 9 8 7 6 5 4 3 2 1

CONTENTS

INTRODUCTION

"Would you like to know the great drama of my life? It is that I have put my genius into my life—I have put only my talent into my works."[1]

Before Lady Gaga, Madonna, Prince, David Bowie, Salvador Dali, or Liberace, there was Oscar Wilde, the archetype of the artist *poseur*. Wilde's character, Lord Henry, may provide a modern motto: "[T]here is only one thing in the world worse than being talked about, and that is not being talked about."

If Wilde had a forerunner, it was Lord Byron, littérateur and scandalous *bon vivant* . . . perhaps one even finds a subtle hint of the charming speech, profligate luxury, and scofflaw in David's son, Absalom. Like Absalom, Wilde's

---

1. Oscar Wilde speaking to André Gide, recorded in *British Authors of the Nineteenth Century*, ed. Stanley Kunitz and Howard Haycraft (New York: H. W. Wilson, 1936), 658.

subversive chatter and consequent actions brought him a sudden reversal, snared by the symbol of his own strength and luxury. Oscar Wilde's career established a cult of artistic spectacle and personal scandal inspiring provocateurs in every generation since.

THE WORLD AROUND

"The dinner table was Wilde's event and made him the greatest talker of his time." [2]

Due to the economic boom England enjoyed (with the consequent moral temptations riches often bring) and the Romantic spirit's resurgence after perhaps an over-measure of hard-nosed capital sense, the late Victorian period was a breeding ground for the not-at-all-starving artist. The philosophical salons of the 17th and 18th centuries receded before the slightly more democratic and often bohemian ideals of artistic enclaves. These were still elite and aristocratically funded, but they were more directly interested in turning cultural tides than many salons of old had been. Generally, this took the form of

---

2. W. B. Yeats on Oscar Wilde in *Autobiographies*, vol. 3 of *The Collected Works of W.B. Yeats*, ed. William H. O'Donnell and Douglas N. Archibald (New York Scribner, 1999), 130.

antagonism to cultural norms. Ironically, the suburban development (that oft-parodied social institution) may trace its origins back to Victorian-era Bedford Park, London, where the likes of W. B. Yeats, Ezra Pound, Thomas Hardy, Henry James, Joseph Conrad, Ford Madox Ford, D. H. Lawrence, and G. K. Chesterton shared their artistic visions in community. So their thoughts and those of John Ruskin, the Pre-Raphaelites, the Aesthetes, and later the Decadents, helped unfold a thousand flowerings of Romantic thought.

One sunflower grew so much larger and seedier than the others; one lily bloomed briefly brighter: but was its whiteness shining the pure heat of artistic genius or broadcasting the pallor of disease and decay? That strange flower was Oscar Wilde.

ABOUT THE AUTHOR

"He looked like a Roman Emperor of the decadence; he was over six feet in height and both broad and thick set . . . his hands were flabby, greasy; his skin looked bilious and dirty . . . . But his grey eyes were finely expressive; in turn vivacious, laughing, sympathetic; always beautiful."[3]

Oscar Fingal O'Flahertie Wills Wilde was born in Dublin, Ireland on October 16, 1854 to the intellectual household of William and Jane Wilde. Both his parents were well-known in their day (William as a doctor and writer; Jane as a poet and political agitator). Oscar distinguished himself studying classics and language (German, French, Greek), garnering top positions and scholarships to Trinity College, Dublin, and then Magdalene College, Oxford, where Wilde graduated with a Newdigate Prize for

---

3. The journalist Frank Harris describes Oscar Wilde. *British Authors of the Nineteenth Century*, 130.

Poetry and First Class honors. Yet, for all the apparent advantages, there were many cracks in the family edifice. William Wilde's affairs, Jane Wilde's political agitation, Willie Wilde's (Oscar's older brother) alcoholic dissipation, and Oscar Wilde's own notorious indiscretions all led to scandal and eventual poverty.

While earning academic honors in college, Oscar Wilde chose a moral path common to many philosophers, artists, and academic cognoscenti: the great ones lived by their own lights, heedless of the trite social and moral boundaries observed by common people. He grew his hair long, decorated his room with a deliberately unmanly flair (flowers, feathers, etc.), and projected an attitude of lazy luxury: "I find it harder and harder every day to live up to my blue china." Wilde made a name for himself as an eccentric wit and reveled in the company of dandy young men, trouncing cultural taboos and tending in his affect to project sympathy and support for the "love that dare not speak its name."[4] He held high court at any dinner table or gathering, astonishing observers with his incredible persona.

After graduation, he toured America (1882), lecturing on art and design, where he received great attention, ridicule, and admiration for his clever words and precocious thoughts. In 1884, he married Constance Lloyd, and though they enjoyed an annual allowance of reasonable

---

4. Generally taken as a euphemism for homosexuality. The phrase was penned by Alfred Douglas in a poem to Wilde.

means, they far outspent it. They soon had children (two sons), but marriage proved challenging for Wilde, and he took to male lovers, sealing an unhappy fate for the couple. Though he had written some shorter pieces, Wilde's first major writing position was as an editor of a women's magazine. Finally, in 1891, he published his one (and only) novel: *The Picture of Dorian Gray.*[5] Wilde then wrote for the theater between 1892 and 1895, the zenith of his career. His chief works were *Lady Windermere's Fan*, *A Woman of No Importance*, *An Ideal Husband*, and *The Importance of Being Earnest*. Up to this point, Wilde's sparkling intelligence and bold posing brought him a wide audience and considerable success; Fortune seemed his to dictate. Yet, how fickle Fortune's friendship is!

Wilde carried on a homosexual affair for some time with the young Lord Alfred Douglas; Douglas's irate father began harassing Wilde over the impropriety, even publicly accusing him of sodomy (illegal at the time, though not generally enforced). Wilde, rather than cut off the relationship, sued Lord Alfred's father for libel. Wilde then had the legal burden of proving himself innocent, which he failed to do (his own works were read as testimony against him; when the prosecution appeared to have male prostitutes he frequented ready to testify, he finally dropped the suit). The failed suit bankrupted Wilde and led immediately to further legal jeopardy when the crown

---

5. He had already published a briefer version of the novel in 1890 in America by serial installment in *Lippincott's Monthly Magazine*.

brought charges against Wilde of sodomy and gross indecency. Found guilty, he was sentenced to two years of prison; there he wrote his famous philosophical letter, published posthumously, "*De Profundis.*"

Wilde emerged from prison a socially notorious, physically broken, and financially ruined man. Estranged from his own wife and children, he wrote very little and relocated to France. His last days were spent in a Parisian hotel after an ear infection escalated into fatal meningitis. He is said to have converted to Catholicism days before his death[6] and finally passed away November 30, 1900, at age 46.

---

6. Actually, he had intended to become Roman Catholic in his early twenties, even scheduling a baptism, but he waffled. His father's threat of cutting off funds and his mentors' words against his religious inclinations may have encouraged his doubts. In the end, he sent the priest a bunch of altar lilies in his stead.

WHAT OTHER
NOTABLES SAID

"Though the Philistines may jostle, you will rank as an apostle in the high aesthetic band, / If you walk down Piccadilly with a poppy or a lily in your mediaeval hand." ~ W. S. Gilbert (obliquely referring to Wilde in the comic opera *Patience*)

"No, I've never cared for [Wilde's] work. Too scented." ~ Rudyard Kipling

"[Wilde] made dying Victorianism laugh at itself, and it may be said to have died of the laughter." ~ Richard Le Gallienne

"Wilde himself wrote some things that were not immorality, but merely bad taste; not the bad taste of the conservative suburbs, which merely means anything violent or shocking, but real bad taste; as

in a stern subject treated in a florid style; an over-
dressed woman at a supper of old friends; or a bad
joke that nobody had time to laugh at. This mixture
of sensibility and coarseness in the man was very
curious; and I for one cannot endure (for example)
his sensual way of speaking of dead substances,
satin or marble or velvet, as if he were stroking a lot
of dogs and cats." ~ G. K. Chesterton

"Am reading more of Oscar Wilde. What a tire-
some, affected sod." ~ Noel Coward

"Oscar turned his words into gems and flung them
to the moon!" ~ Herbert Beerbohm Tree

"Rather like Gore Vidal in our time, Wilde was
able to be mordant and witty because he was, deep
down and on the surface, *un homme serieux*. May his
memory stay carnation-green. May he ever encour-
age us to think that the bores and the bullies and
the literal minds need not always win. May he in-
duce us to rise from our semi-recumbent postures."[7]
~ Christopher Hitchens

---

7. From Hitchens's work *Unacknowledged Legislation: Writers in the
Public Sphere* (London: Verso, 2000), 9.

PLOT SUMMARY, SETTING, AND CHARACTERS

- *Setting: London, England in the late nineteenth century (the narrative indicates that Dorian also travels abroad, but the central action takes place in Victorian London)*
- *Dorian Gray:* Gray was born to a rich world of pride and leisure. His mother (Margaret Devereux) married for love, angering her wealthy father, Lord Kelso, who caused the death of her husband (paying a man to duel the hated husband). Margaret died soon afterward herself. Dorian, orphaned, is raised by Kelso, who hates to look upon the boy, but provides for him generously when he comes of age. Young Dorian (his age is never stated, but we can imagine him about eighteen or twenty years old at the outset of the novel) is gloriously handsome and sits

for a painted portrait by Basil Hallward, who is just putting the finishing touches on the canvas when the novel opens. Gray is the Faustian character Wilde wrote that he "would like to be—in other ages, perhaps."[8]

- *Basil Hallward:* an artist. A certain Lady Brandon introduces Hallward to the young Dorian Gray. Hallward finds artistic inspiration in the aesthetic perfection of the young man and has Dorian sit for a full-length portrait. It is Hallward's finest work, and he gives it to Dorian as a gift when complete. Wilde thought Basil Hallward the nearest in character to himself.

- *Lord Henry Wotton:* Lord Henry is a young example (only ten years older than Dorian) of Mephistophelean wickedness. He soaks in illicit pleasures and encourages others to share the waters with him. Wotton's wife, Victoria, leaves him, and Lord Henry leads Dorian Gray into a life of selfish corruption. Wilde wrote that Wotton was closest to what the world thought of him.

- *Sybil Vane:* A beautiful and talented actress who plays Shakespearean parts for Mr. Isaacs's

---

8. Terence Dawson "Dorian Gray as Symbolic Representation of Wilde's Personality," Victorian Web, last modified on June 8 2007, http://www.victorianweb.org/authors/wilde/dawson16.html (accessed on February 6, 2017).

theater. She falls for Dorian. When she meets the reality of his cold heart, she commits suicide.

- *James Vane:* Sybil's brother; he immediately dislikes Gray and later tracks down Dorian to avenge his sister's tragic death.
- *Alan Campbell, Adrian Singleton:* These and other characters about Dorian Gray are stained or ruined by his influence on them.

The novel opens in Basil Hallward's studio on a beautiful summer day, flower scents wafting in and mixing with Lord Henry Wotton's opium-laced cigarette smoke. Hallward, a painter, is putting the finishing touches on his finest work, a full-length portrait of Dorian Gray. Wotton recognizes the masterly work; the two men take a walk out to the garden, and Hallward explains the background of his meeting and painting of Gray. Wotton is keen on meeting this aesthetic marvel of a young man.

While they are out, Gray enters the studio. The two older men return and greet Dorian. Lord Henry Wotton and Gray then take a turn conversing in the garden while Hallward puts a few final touches on the canvas. Gray is drawn to the sense of worldly knowledge radiating from Wotton, and is caught by Wotton's dark words, "When your youth goes, your beauty will go with it, and then you will suddenly discover that there are no triumphs left for you .... You will become sallow, and hollow-cheeked, and dull-eyed. You will suffer horribly" (22).

When they return to the studio, Hallward has finished, and all agree that it is his finest work. Hallward then gives the portrait to Gray, but Dorian seems moodily stunned: "'How sad it is!' murmured Dorian Gray with his eyes still fixed upon his own portrait. 'How sad it is! I shall grow old, and horrible, and dreadful. But this picture will remain always young…. If it were only the other way! If it were I who was to be always young, and the picture that was to grow old…. I would give my soul for that!'" (2.25-26). Wotton's poisonous words, then, serve as the inciting incident as the infected Dorian, wishing for the strange blessing, calls down a curse upon himself: his pristine youth will remain intact, sin and age's tarnishing will only visit the canvas.

At first, no character knows that the fateful transaction has actually taken place. Dorian Gray draws nearer and nearer Lord Henry Wotton, and Wotton spins his webs of enchantment over his protégé, as they descend into ever-growing cynicism and sin. Dorian takes a liking to Sibyl Vane, an actress, and she is entirely charmed and enchanted—too much so. She falters in her acting, and Dorian attacks her for it (her performance embarrassed him; he had brought others to showcase her talent). She is heart-broken. When Gray arrives at him home, he notices a marked change in the portrait, a "touch of cruelty in the mouth." Gray, realizing the curse, immediately writes an apology letter, though he does not love her. But it is too late: she has committed suicide. The news comes by (of course) Lord Wotton, who persuades Gray to attend the opera with him rather than mourn the loss of Vane.

Dorian Gray, staying his fiendish course, decides to cover the portrait. Basil Hallward visits, hoping to borrow the painting for an exhibition, but Gray angrily refuses him even the sight of the work. Gray then hides the painting in an old attic schoolroom he had often been locked away in as a child.

Wotton further seduces Gray's mind with scandalous literature, which Gray digests greedily. The two (Gray and Wotton) spend time abroad together, but Dorian returns occasionally to see the steady degeneration of cursed canvas. This continues for some eighteen years. Dorian Gray's name becomes a byword for scandal, and Basil Hallward visits. Dorian decides to show him the canvas, and Hallward, shocked, begs Dorian to join him in repenting of their idolatries.

Instead, Gray is overcome with murderous zeal and stabs Hallward to death. Gray then blackmails a scientific acquaintance to dissolve the corpse in chemicals. As with the earlier crimes, Gray appears to feel momentary compunction, but then carries on his wicked way. James Vane, Sybil's brother, seeks revenge on Dorian, but believes Gray's lie that he has mistaken his man when he looks closely at his face . . . how could an almost forty-year-old appear so young? Later Vane is hiding in the forest for Gray while Dorian is out in a hunting party; Vane is mistaken for game and shot dead.

Dorian Gray wonders if he can begin to reverse the hideous curse with good deeds; therefore, he spares a poor young lady he was near to ruining . . . but upon checking the portrait, it is only worse: "He could see no change, save that in the eyes there was a look of cunning and in the mouth the curved wrinkle of the hypocrite. The thing was still loathsome—more loathsome, if possible, than before." Taking the knife he used to murder Basil Howard, Dorian Gray stabs the portrait. A horrific cry followed by a crash draw the servants, but they cannot break down the door. Finally gaining entry by a balcony, they find the portrait of young Dorian Gray perfect and intact, and an old man lying dead—a knife in his heart—"wrinkled, withered, and loathsome of visage." Only after examining his rings do they identify the villain.

WORLDVIEW ANALYSIS

"As a matter of fact I do not think that one person influences another, nor do I think there is a bad influence in the world."[9]

Sometimes an idea is so clearly misguided that only the smitten and ingenuous can receive it. The italicized quote above, taken from Wilde's court testimony, is such a statement and stands entirely on the grandstanding hubris of the speaker. Handled in the clear light of day, the idea is engaging largely because of its bold absurdity. It may serve as a fitting culmination of so much that Wilde did and said; a moment to recognize his worldview caught far outside its native province of card tables, velvet jackets, dining engagements, and sly characters. We begin with reflection on this phrase and its consequences, then treat its significance to the novel.

---

9. Oscar Wilde, from his courtroom testimony, see *The Picture of Dorian Gray: Norton Critical Edition* (New York: W. W. Norton, 1988), 360.

Does one person influence another? Of course! From the cradle to the grave, there may be no more evident fact about human behavior than the fact that our lives are inextricably bound to others. We must, or how would a toddler even learn to walk or speak? As we mature, we grow more careful in our imitation, more discrete in adopting those traits we admire, but the natural human inclination to imitate what it loves and reject what it hates stays with us all to the grave. Is it possible to suffer a bad influence from another person? Again, the answer is only too clear, and one need only consider pivotal relationships in one's life to verify the truth.

So, why would Oscar Wilde make such a remark? First, it fits in with his overall pose of provocative artist and aesthete. No doubt, an audible gasp—and chuckle—rippled over the courtroom more than once during those trials when Wilde took the witness stand.

Second, don't forget that Wilde was exceptionally intelligent; he had good reason to say such a thing.[10] Beside the stirring effect, Wilde had a larger context in mind: if one person cannot corrupt another, how could he have sexually corrupted Alfred Douglas? Thus, there should be no case made against Wilde, nor should his works be repressed due to perceived illicit content. If Wilde could

---

10. For the complete court transcript, see the University of Missouri: http://law2.umkc.edu/faculty/projects/ftrials/wilde/Wildelibeltranowcross.html (accessed on February 6, 2017).

successfully unhinge moral connections from people and their words, he would be free to do and write as he wished.

One of the abiding ironies of the court drama is that of all the works one might have used against Oscar Wilde, the crown chose *The Picture of Dorian Gray* . . . the one work that showcases Victorian morality in such an obvious and ironclad manner that Wilde himself blushed. Read his own defense of the novel, written five years before the trial: "The painter, Basil Hallward, worshiping beauty far too much, as most painters do, dies by the hand of the one in whose soul he has created a monstrous and absurd vanity. Dorian Gray, having led a life of mere sensation and pleasure, tires to kill conscience, and that moment kills himself . . . . Yes; there is a terrible moral in *Dorian Gray*—a moral which the prurient will not be able to find in it, but which will be revealed to all whose minds are healthy. Is it an artistic error? I fear it is. It is the only error in the book." Yet, is this the very book read to Wilde in court to prove his immorality?

The world took the wicked words of Lord Henry Wotton as Wilde's own beliefs. Generally, an author and his characters enjoy liberty to see the world independently, and failing to allow a separation is a serious interpretive flaw. Certainly, Wilde's manner and reputation made the conflation tempting, and, though Wilde points out that Wotton is eventually wounded as a mere "spectator" to Dorian Gray's downfall, he is the one central character who survives the Gothic horror before us. Also, the court wasn't concerned so much with what Oscar Wilde meant as what other impressionable readers (like Alfred Douglas) might reasonably interpret from the flashing phrases and winsome evil of Wotton. So, the one work that Wilde thought stained by simplistic morality happened to be the book some looked to chiefly when seeking to determine Wilde's own immorality.

Strangely, rather than rely on the evident morality of the novel, explaining it to the court, Wilde argued that there are no bad influences and that artists have no moral or ethical boundaries that they should or must observe in their work. He entered the courtroom, suing a man for declaring society's open secret. He entered jail refusing to explain or defend the morality he penned in the closing pages of *Dorian Gray*.[11]

Now, with the court quotation in the back of our minds, let's consider the key word that arises in *Dorian Gray*'s opening chapters, the central word that affects every aspect of characterization, plot, and theme to the closing scene: *influence*. The word Wilde discounted in court actually established the architecture of his masterful novel.

Consider the words of Basil Hallward concerning Dorian Gray (emphasis added) as he talks at length with Lord Wotton:

---

11. Wilde's narrator states that "Dorian Gray had been poisoned by a book," a moral idea Wilde certainly would wish to avoid in his court case; that, too, may have caused Wilde to seek a moral perspective in opposition to that presented in his novel.

- "[Dorian] is all my art to me now .... [H]is personality has suggested to me an entirely new manner in art .... I see things differently, I think of them differently. I can now recreate life in a way that was hidden from me before .... Some subtle *influence* passed from him to me, and for the first time in my life I saw in the plain woodland the wonder I had always looked for, and always missed" (14).

- "As long as I live, the personality of Dorian Gray will dominate me" (16).

- "Don't spoil him. Don't try to *influence* him. Your *influence* would be bad" (17).

Or take this exchange between Dorian and Wotton:

- Gray: "Have you really a very bad *influence*, Lord Henry?"

- Wotton: "There is no such thing as a good *influence*, Mr. Gray. All *influence* is immoral—immoral from the scientific point of view.... Because to *influence* a person is to give him one's own soul" (19).

As Wotton's clever epigrams and calculated remarks pile up, worming through Dorian's mind, Dorian becomes entranced: "For nearly ten minutes [Dorian] stood there, motionless, with parted lips, and eyes strangely bright. He was dimly conscious that entirely fresh *influences* were at work within him" (20). Wotton "with his subtle smile . . . watched him. He knew the precise psychological moment when to say nothing . . . . He was amazed at the sudden impression that his words had produced [on Dorian Gray]" (21).

Thus, the novel hinges on influence, of the serpent in the garden variety. What is Dorian's influence on Hallward? Lord Wotton's influence on Dorian? Dorian's influence on the painting? The painting's influence on Dorian? *The Picture of Dorian Gray* is a dark tracing of influences and their consequences.

Two sinister influences that drive the novel are 1) an idolatrous view of certain people, and 2) an idolatrous view of art. Hallward's idolatry of Dorian Gray and Dorian's idolatry of Lord Wotton and his clever worldview are established above. Simultaneously, those conversations reveal a view of art as religion. Without belaboring the point, Basil Hallward betrays a suspect artistic perspective when he exclaims, "There is nothing that Art cannot express . . . . Dorian Gray is to me simply a motive in art . . . I see everything in him. He is never more present in my work than when no image of him is there . . . I have put into [the portrait] some expression of all this curious artistic idolatry" (15). Hallward recognizes his view of Dorian and the consequent artistic expression as "idolatry," yet he will not consider what trouble this false worship may bring. Wotton and Gray also misuse art, chiefly as a means of escape from moral reality (after a great sin, such as driving Sibyl to suicide, they rush off to the opera and other delights to beguile their hearts and consciences into complacency).

The personal and artistic idolatry join to conceive the monstrous curse of the idolized man (Dorian Gray) demonically energizing the work of the artist's hand (the portrait). In this sense, we have a Gothic horror in the vein of Mary Shelley (*Frankenstein*), Edgar Allan Poe ("The Masque of the Red Death"), or D. H. Lawrence ("The Rocking-Horse Winner"). Dorian Gray is infected by Lord Wotton's philosophy: "Youth! Youth! There is absolutely nothing in the world but youth!" (24). Believing this lie, Gray desires a life of perpetual youth untroubled by moral realities. And his desire, his prayer, yields a cursed life for him and those around him. The Apostle James is certainly right: "When desire has conceived, it gives birth to sin; and sin, when it is full-grown, brings forth death" (1:15). Or from Deuteronomy, "Cursed is anyone who makes an idol—a thing detestable to the LORD, the work of skilled hands—and sets it up in secret" (NIV, 27:15). Fittingly, as Basil Hallward's theory of art developed, he also claims, "I have grown to love secrecy," unwilling to divulge the source of his inspiration to others (9). Likewise, Dorian keeps his idolatrous record of wrongs covered and hidden in the attic. Like so many sins, the idol is set up "in secret," but the effects will eventually become public.

Once the opening idolatry establishes the unholy mir-
acle of the portrait, there can be no other conclusion but
destruction, following a traditional moral cause and effect
of influence in *The Picture of Dorian Gray*. In the final chapter, Dorian Gray hopes to change his course and resolves
to do so (though he is too late). He even warns Wotton of
wicked influences: "You poisoned me with a book once. I
should not forgive that. Harry, promise me that you will
never lend that book to any one. It does harm" (278). If the
novel is a degrading or immoral book (as many in Wilde's
day claimed[12]), it is certainly not because it lacks a clear
moral in the central storyline.

So, how is it that so many claimed that this novel was
contemptible? One reasonable moral objection to the
novel parallels the manner a wayward Christian shares his
testimony, reveling in the excitement and enticements of
his prodigal years over the salvation of his own soul by
God, exposing hypocritical sympathies. The subtle insin-
uation of possible homosexual attraction among the main
characters (which was more directly stated in early drafts),

---

12. Upon publication in 1890, English critics attacked *The Picture of
Dorian Gray* on two major fronts: composition (both structural and
philosophical) and moral implications. The *St. James's Gazette* quipped:
"a very lame story it is, and very lamely told," not so much "dangerous
and corrupt" as "incurably silly .... mere catchpenny revelations of the
non-existent" (334). The *Daily Chronicle* called it "a tale spawned from
the leprous literature of the French *Décadents*—a poisonous book, the
atmosphere of which is heavy with mephitic odours of moral and spir-
itual putrefaction" (342-343).

the languorously scented air hanging over every page, and the facetious philosophies furthered throughout Wotton's lines triggered a response from conservative readers who instinctively knew what dark fruits the "New Hedonists" would soon be bringing forth as moral capital was quickly depleting in England. Lord Wotton's deliciously clever words dominate so many conversations,[13] and Wilde's wittiest arts are spent on his behalf, so the reader may suspect that the concluding moral is a cover granting Wilde free reign for Lord Henry Wotton's scandalous thoughts. This line of thought is further supported by the fact that

---

13   One of the most pernicious ideas that Wotton purveys concerns temptation and sin: "[S]elf-denial mars our lives. We are punished for our refusals. Every impulse that we strive to strangle broods in the mind, and poisons us . . . . The only way to get rid of a temptation is to yield to it. Resist it, and your soul grows sick with longing" (20). He holds out no hope for the struggling sinner except in an unrestrained embrace of passion, calling poisonous the very things God's Word prescribes for our health ("flee youthful lusts", "resist the Devil and he will flee from you", "consider it all joy when you face various trials, knowing that the testing of your faith produces patience"). Dorian begins his journey to his death after this misleading discourse. Wotton's philosophy is inherently self-centered: "The aim of life is self-development. To realize one's nature perfectly—that is what each of us is here for" (19). But the truth is that our nature is fallen, so the full realization of that nature—embracing everything we desire—will destroy us, as it does Hallward and Gray. Christians are to be vigilant, "taking every thought captive to make it obedient to Christ"; Wotton certainly keeps the thoughtful warrior busy.

Wilde seemed ashamed of the morality in the novel, calling it the only "error" in the text.

On the other hand, as the chapters proceed, the reader is given no indication that Lord Henry's musings have much reliable truth in them; quite the contrary. In fact, whenever Dorian Gray decadently follows Wotton's advice to embrace a tempting passion, he simply appears vile. His verbal treatment of Sibyl Vane is so grossly vain, self-centered, and petty, it's nearly impossible to read. And the dialogue never rings out more clearly than when Basil Hallward confronts the horror of the curse: "Good God, Dorian, what a lesson! what an awful lesson! . . . Pray, Dorian, pray . . . 'Lead us not into temptation. Forgive us our sins. Wash away our iniquities.' Let us say that together. The prayer of your pride has been answered. The prayer of your repentance will be answered also. I worshiped you too much. I am punished for it. You worshiped yourself too much. We are both punished . . . . It is never too late, Dorian. Let us kneel down and try if can cannot remember a prayer" (122-123). But Hallward's honest words only further enrage Dorian to murderously silence the repentant, preaching artist. Again, Gray appears a fiendish, sick excuse for a human being, lacking any manly loyalty or kindness. Wotton's selfish philosophies and foolish advice to embrace every temptation prove lethal. In the end, Wotton is unaware of the monster that Gray has become, for Wotton attends only to superficial beauty. Wotton's erstwhile clever remarks fall flat and lifeless, chapter by chapter, one by one, as the novel marches to its horrific conclusion. Thus, one cannot make a good case for the moral simply being stamped on to excuse Wotton's words.

Today, despite any dangers that the atmosphere, philosophy, and insinuations pose to simple-minded reading, the novel is not to be overlooked in contempt. Consider that there may be a perverse sexual desire in a human being; or that people may believe lies, spin them forth in clever ways, and tempt others by them; or that our art and social environments may be saturated with moral escapism and inducements to evil. These are the obvious conditions the modern reader confronts daily, and Wilde's novel reflects the fruit these conditions engender: despair and death. Moreover, while the atmosphere is dark and twisted, Wilde does not linger in any explicit detail over the sinful actions of his characters; nor does Wilde cause the stated sins and immorality to appear winsome or lastingly enjoyable. So, though the work was scandalous in its day, the novel should not be classified with lewd or perverse literature then or since.

Rather than avoid this literary parable, the mature reader has much to learn from Dorian Gray and Wilde himself: many idols to topple, many swords to sharpen, many thoughts to take captive; only go well armed when encountering the novel's early worldly charms. By the final chapters, the reader should encounter a truth that may prove a good influence after all: We steward a soul, a gift from God; it rises or falls in the purity, grace, and honesty whereby we honor God with our highest worship. So permit no other person or created thing to take that place. On the other hand, ignore the guidance of conscience's promptings, and we run to wretched ruin.

QUOTABLES

Preface

1. The artist is the creator of beautiful things. To reveal art and conceal the artist is art's aim.

2. There is no such thing as a moral or an immoral book. Books are well written, or badly written. That is all.

3. The only excuse for making a useless thing is that one admires it intensely. All art is quite useless.

Lord Henry Wotton

4. I like persons better than principles, and I like persons with no principles better than anything else in the world.

5. Laughter is not at all a bad beginning for a friendship, and it is far the best ending for one.

6.   Nothing can cure the soul but the senses, just as nothing can cure the senses but the soul.

7.   To me, beauty is the wonder of wonders. It is only shallow people who do not judge by appearances. The true mystery of the world is the visible, not the invisible.

8.   Nowadays most people die of a sort of creeping common sense, and discover when it is too late that the only things one never regrets are one's mistakes.

9.   The real drawback to marriage is that it makes one unselfish. And unselfish people are colourless.

10. As for a spoiled life, no life is spoiled but one whose growth is arrested. If you want to mar a nature, you have merely to reform it.

11. Pleasure is Nature's test, her sign of approval. When we are happy, we are always good, but when we are good, we are not always happy.

12. Women . . . inspire us with the desire to do masterpieces, and always prevent us from carrying them out.

13. We live in an age when unnecessary things are our only necessities.

14. It is perfectly monstrous the way people go about nowadays saying things against one behind one's back that are absolutely and entirely true.

15. I admit that I think that it is better to be beautiful than to be good.

16. To get back my youth I would do anything in the world, except take exercise, get up early, or be respectable.

17. [To Dorian Gray] You are the type of what the age is searching for, and what it is afraid it has found. I'm so glad that you have never...produced anything outside of yourself! Life has been your art. You have set yourself to music.

Basil Hallward

18. Sin is a thing that writes itself across a man's face. It cannot be concealed. People talk sometimes of secret vices. There are no such things. If a wretched man has a vice, it shows itself in the lines of his mouth, the droop of his eyelids, the moulding of his hands even.

Dorian Gray

19. You have explained me to myself, Harry .... How well you know me!

20. I love scandals about other people, but scandals about me don't interest me. They have not got the charm of novelty.

21. [Preparing to reveal the hideous portrait to Hallward]
    I will show you my soul. You shall see the thing that
    you fancy only God can see.

22. Each of us has heaven and hell in him.

Third-Person Omniscient Narrator

23. There is always something ridiculous about the emo-
    tions of people whom one has ceased to love.

24. What the worm was to the corpse, his sins would be to
    the painted image on the canvas. They would mar its
    beauty and eat away its grace. They would defile it and
    make it shameful. And yet the thing would still live on.
    It would be always alive.

25. Dorian Gray had been poisoned by a book. There were
    moments when he looked on evil simply as a mode
    through which he could realize his conception of the
    beautiful.

26. It was his beauty that had ruined him, his beauty and
    the youth that he had prayed for. But for those two
    things, his life might have been free from stain. His
    beauty had been to him but a mask, his youth but a
    mockery. What was youth at best? A green, an unripe
    time, a time of shallow moods, and sickly thoughts.
    Why had he worn its livery? Youth had spoiled him.

21 SIGNIFICANT QUESTIONS AND ANSWERS

1. Preface: If you could imagine one of the characters in *The Picture of Dorian Gray* writing the novel's preface, which character's voice and sentiments would you choose?

   > Lord Henry Wotton's voice is nearest the pithy, aesthetically focused style of Wilde in the preface.

2. What do you make of the final statement in the Preface that "All art is quite useless." Do you agree with this? Do you think Oscar Wilde being sincere? What evidence can you bring to support the idea that Wilde is or is not being sincere?

   > Answers will vary. The statement reminds the reader that a particular artwork may not serve a specific use that society wishes for it, but it is absurd to believe that all art has no use. The use may be for moral

edification or financial improvement; it may be fame, vanity, enjoyment, or simply a sense of personal accomplishment, but mankind has found many uses for art.

3. Ch. 1: Find one statement in chapter 1 that is simply not true. Explain why it is not true.

> Example: "Conscience and cowardice are really the same things." As with most things Lord Wotton quips, this is obviously false, and the reader should get used to confronting (and chuckling over) his froth. The conclusion of the novel shows this to be false; as Dorian Gray seeks to hide his sin, too cowardly to confess, he decides to kill his conscience. Thus, it would be truthful to say that a good conscience and bravery are closer relations.

4. Ch. 2: Why does the painting upset Dorian? How does he act?

> The painting can keep its youthful charm, but he must lose his. Dorian acts sullenly. But when Hallward moves to cut the canvas with a knife, Dorian jumps to save it, claiming that act would be "murder."

5. Ch. 4: Who has Dorian become infatuated with?

> Sibyl Vane, an actress. He has proposed marriage to her.

6. Ch. 7: What happens to undo the couple's happiness? What does Gray notice in the painting?

> Sibyl performs badly and Dorian attacks and abuses her verbally, stating that she "killed love" by her "third-rate [acting]." Later, he sees that the picture has changed; he can detect a cruelty in the lips that was not present before. Wondering, he decides to repent his words to her, to write her a letter and repair the relationship.

7. Ch. 8: What happened to Sibyl Vane?

> Gray's fierce words wounded her so badly that she decided to commit suicide by swallowing poison before his letter reached her. Dorian and Wotton go to the opera.

8. What are ways that people around us seek to escape a troubled conscience? What is the best thing to do when our conscience is troubled?

> Answers will vary. Evading a guilty conscience always involves some form of deceit (private and public) to hide the fact that our consciences bear witness to the law when we break it (Rom. 2:14–15). Similarly, like Dorian, unrepentant sinners must "sear" their consciences to make them insensitive (1 Tim. 4:2). Peace comes from drawing near to God, who cleanses a guilty conscience (Heb. 9:14; 10:22), and to the Bible, which helps a troubled conscience see the truth clearly (2 Cor. 4:2; 1 Tim. 3:9).

9.   Ch. 9: What does Basil Hallward want? How does
     Gray respond? Why?

     Hallward wants to borrow the portrait, but Gray
     refuses. Gray also refuses to sit for another portrait.
     Dorian Gray is afraid that his sin will be revealed.

10. Ch. 11: What are some of the diversions Gray is pursu-
     ing? What is the effect?

     Answers will vary; there are many. The end result
     is boredom, and he returns to the opera, watching
     Tannhäuser because he sees in it the "tragedy of his
     own soul."

11. Can you think of ways that people in our culture, even
     while running away from a troubled conscience, actual-
     ly fixate upon the very sins they fear to confess?

     One can see in so many stories/movies/songs of
     violence, deceit, and the like, people somehow seek-
     ing to explore their troubled conscience through
     art. While art can play midwife, people need to
     go the Lord for true wisdom, understanding, and
     forgiveness.

12. Ch. 13: What happens when Basil Hallward finally
     sees his masterpiece?

     He recognizes the curse that appears to be a
     blessing (Dorian's untarnished appearance, despite
     his worst thoughts and deeds). He recognizes that

both he and Dorian had made an idol of Dorian's youth and beauty, and he calls on Dorian to kneel and repent with him, quoting the Lord's prayer, the Catholic mass, and Isaiah.

13. When someone has discovered a lie or other sin in your life, were you ever tempted to hate that person, even though the sin was yours? What happened? Have you reconciled with that person?

    Answers will vary.

14. Ch. 14: What does Dorian Gray do with Basil Hallward's body?

    He blackmails an acquaintance, Alan Campbell, to dissolve the body in chemicals.

15. Ch. 15: That same night, Gray goes off to a party, and "for a moment felt keenly the terrible pleasure of a double life." Did Oscar Wilde know what it felt like to live a double life? Explain.

    Answers will vary. Oscar Wilde certainly knew a double life. At the very least, maintaining a public marriage while simultaneously carrying on several other intimate relationships is a matter of grave duplicity.

16. Ch. 16–17: How does Gray escape the revenge of James Vane (Sibyl's brother)?

He shows Vane how young he looks; he could not
possibly be eighteen years older than on the day of
her death. Later, Vane is accidentally shot by hunt-
ers while he is hiding in the forest.

17. Dorian finally tries to do good and reverse his curse.
    Why does it do no good that he spares ruining the
    young woman, Hetty?

    He is only acting out of another kind of self-love.
    Apparently, the highest love he can now aspire to is
    merely hypocritical.

18. Does any character act in a heroic manner in the course
    of the novel? Is there any character you esteem at any
    point? Explain.

    Answers will vary. Basil Hallward, when he rec-
    ognizes his and Dorian's mutual sin and calls for
    repentance, shows courage and heroism before he
    is murdered.

19. In the end, the book is not really about the best artistic
    or aesthetic philosophy. What is the moral heart of the
    novel?

    The novel concerns the life and death of one char-
    acter's conscience, one soul who trusted in (Lord
    Wotton's) lies.

20. What is the difference between the soul and the conscience? What are specific ways that you can better steward your own conscience and soul?

> Your soul is your living self that will live on into eternity. God breathed life into you, granting you an ever-living soul. We speak of aspects of our soul (such as mind, heart, conscience, or reason); these are not independent organs of the soul but terms that help us consider various facets or operations of our soul. The conscience may refer to a group ("the conscience of America") or an individual[14] and is an inner moral knowledge helping us judge right from wrong, bringing conviction. The Bible says that our conscience can be bothered, seared, defiled, and blinded when yoked to a corrupt heart enslaved to sin, but it can also be purged, cleansed, peaceful, pure, and good when we are renewed in Christ and walk in the light.

21. Do you see an parallels between any character in the novel and Oscar Wilde's own life? Explain.

> Answers will vary, but should reference the many parallels provided throughout this guide.

---

14. "[H]ow much more shall the blood of Christ, who through the eternal Spirit offered Himself without spot to God, cleanse your conscience from dead works to serve the living God?" (Heb. 9:14)

FURTHER DISCUSSION
AND REVIEW

Master what you have read by reviewing and integrating the different elements of this classic.

SETTING AND CHARACTERS

Be able to compare and contrast the personalities (including strengths, weaknesses, and mannerisms) of each character. Which characters change over the course of the novel? Which do not?

PLOT

Be able to describe the beginning, middle, and end of the book along with specific details that move the plot forward and make it compelling. Is the James Vane confrontation part of the main plot or subplot? Literary critic Lawrence Perrine defines climax quite simply: *the turning point or high point in a plot.* But the turning point (the moment the complication begins to resolve) isn't always the moment of highest intensity in a plot. Thus, the climax of a work is a debatable point partly conditioned on which element is in view (turning point or high point). What is the turning point of the novel? What is the moment of highest emotional tension or power? Are they the same point?

CONFLICT

Although we note plenty of external conflict (betrayal, murder, revenge) in the novel, the central conflict is internal. Explain both the internal and external conflicts.

THEME STATEMENTS

Human beings are deeply influenced by others.

Dorian Gray meets the reader as a naïve perfection. He seems a blank slate but is quickly being formed by the mesmerizing and deceptive charm of Lord Henry Wotton. How easily those who seem successful, intelligent, worldly wise, bold, and decadent can captivate our imaginations and lead us astray. Choose companions prudently.

One person or generation may preach a charming lie it doesn't fully understand or live out, while those raised on the lie may live it out more consistently, realizing the consequences to much greater ruin.

This is the case with Lord Wotton (acting as a father figure) and Dorian Gray (his protégé).

Physical beauty is not a reliable measure of inner purity.

Nor is wealth, health, or ease a necessary indication of God's approval of a person (I Tim. 5:24).

There is no way to hide sin indefinitely (Num. 32:23).

When we bury our sin, it grows into the tree from which our conscience hangs mute and lifeless. When we sin, we must confess it, leave it, and make restitution, living honestly before God and man.

When we place something above God, we end up destroying it and ourselves.

Basil Hallward worshiped Dorian Gray, and Dorian Gray worshiped himself; their idolatry brought about their own destruction.

A NOTE FROM THE PUBLISHER:
TAKING THE CLASSICS QUIZ

Once you have finished the worldview guide, you can prepare for the end-of-book test. Each test will consist of a short-answer section on the book itself and the author, a short-answer section on plot and the narrative, and a long-answer essay section on worldview, conflict, and themes.

Each quiz, along with other helps, can be downloaded for free at www.canonpress.com/ClassicsQuizzes. If you have any questions about the quiz or its answers or the Worldview Guides in general, you can contact Canon Press at service@canonpress.com or 208.892.8074.

Marcus Schwager holds a Master's degree in Humanities from California State University, Dominguez Hills, writing his thesis on G. K. Chesterton. He and his wife, Meris, have five children and attend Trinity Covenant Church in Aptos, California. He writes for Canon Press, teaches upper-school Humanities at St. Abraham's Classical Christian Academy, and works for his family's construction and real estate company.

www.ingramcontent.com/pod-product-compliance
Lightning Source LLC
Chambersburg PA
CBHW071934020426
42331CB00010B/2866